To Merret and Harlan,
my heart and my home

A Feiwel and Friends Book

An imprint of Macmillan Publishing Group, LLC
175 Fifth Avenue, New York, NY 10010

Our books may be purchased in bulk for promotional, educational, or business use.
Please contact your local bookseller or the Macmillan Corporate and Premium Sales Department at (800) 221-7945 ext.
5442 or by email at MacmillanSpecialMarkets@macmillan.com.

Library of Congress Cataloging-in-Publication Data

Names: Mundorff, Lisa, author, illustrator.
Title: Welcome home : where nature's most creative creatures dwell / Lisa Mundorff.
Description: First edition. | New York : Feiwel and Friends, 2019.
Identifiers: LCCN 2018039152 | ISBN 978-1-250-21162-0 (hardcover)
Subjects: LCSH: Animals—Habitations—Juvenile literature.
Classification: LCC QL756 .M86 2019 | DDC 591.56/4—dc23
LC record available at https://lccn.loc.gov/2018039152

Book design by Rebecca Syracuse
Feiwel and Friends logo designed by Filomena Tuosto
First Edition, 2019

The art was made by combining sketches and scanned mono prints for
background textures in Photoshop, and was then built digitally.

1 3 5 7 9 10 8 6 4 2

mackids.com

Welcome Home

Where Nature's Most Creative Creatures Dwell

Lisa Mundorff

Feiwel and Friends ● New York

Beavers live in a **lodge**.

An otter's resting place is called a **couch**.

A lion lives in a **den**.

A pig's home is a pigsty.

Red pandas are solitary animals who live in trees.

One could say dolphins live in **pods**, **herds**, or even **teams**.

Pigeons live in **lofts**.

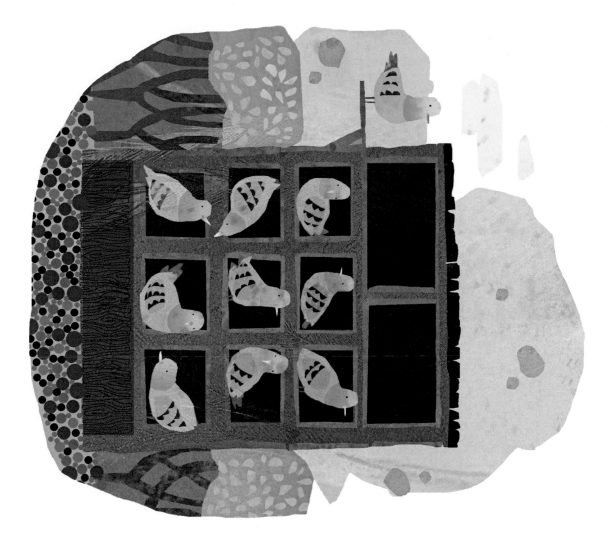

Prairie dogs live in **neighborhoods.**

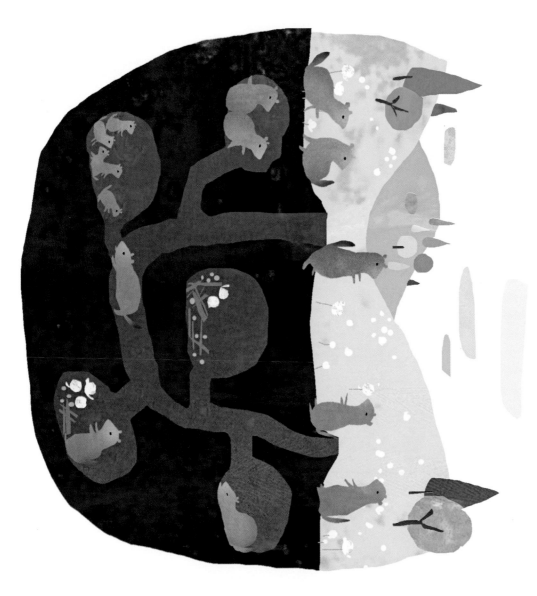

A group of
neighborhoods
becomes a town . . .

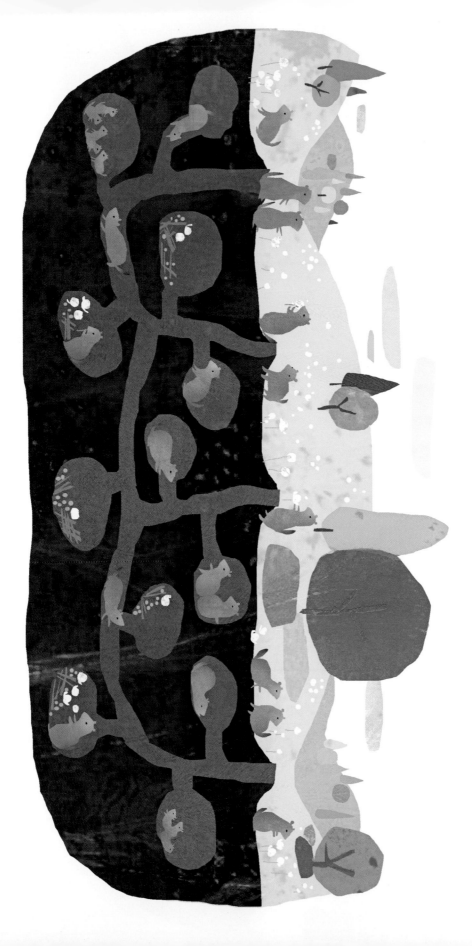

...a **town** on Earth, a place
all creatures call **home**
and live with love.

More Fun Facts

A lion's roar can be heard from up to five miles away.

The pigeon is one of the most intelligent among the bird species.

Prairie dogs say hello with a kiss.

Tigers, foxes, wolves, and coyotes all live in lairs.

Pigs are playful, intelligent, and social animals. They chat with other pigs using more than twenty different vocalizations.

When otters aren't resting on their couches, they love to play. Crafting slides and sliding down them is a favorite activity.

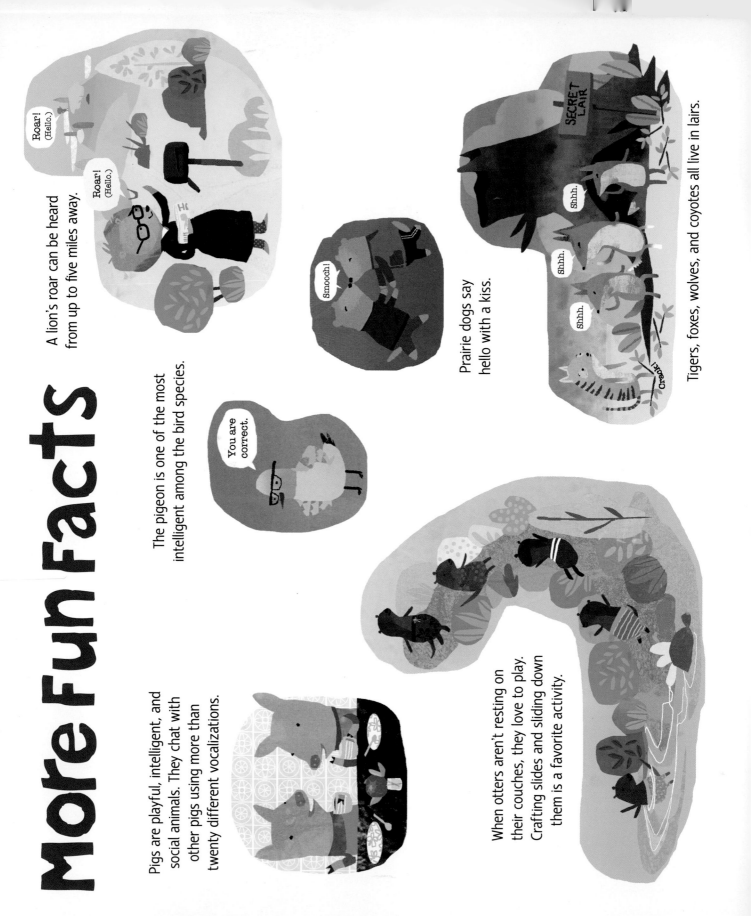

Beavers are monogamous. That means they find their one and only partner and stay with them for a lifetime.

Gorillas, alligators, squirrels, crows, and ducks all live in nests.

The red panda wraps its tail around its body to stay warm at night.

Bears live in caves. So do bats, snails, spiders, and salamanders.

Moles live in fortresses.

An ant lives in a colony. So do penguins and naked mole rats.